T0195836

Night Night Sweet Child

Marlene Yoder

WestBow Press books may be ordered through booksellers or by contacting:

WestBow Press
A Division of Thomas Nelson & Zondervan
1663 Liberty Drive
Bloomington, IN 47403
www.westbowpress.com
844-714-3454

Interior Image Credit: Jolene Yoder

ISBN: 978-1-6642-6622-3 (sc)
ISBN: 978-1-6642-6623-0 (e)

Library of Congress Control Number: 2022908563

Print information available on the last page.

WestBow Press rev. date: 05/17/2022

WestBow
P R E S S®
A DIVISION OF THOMAS NELSON
& ZONDERVAN

Dedication

This book is dedicated to my daughter who always has trouble falling asleep.

Prologue

I've always wanted a book to read to my daughter that would relax her and make her feel confident in herself!

May you read this and find a joyful rest knowing that God is watching over you all night long!

To all the mothers out there with little or no sleep at all, I pray for you! Stay strong! You are not alone! Why not send a prayer for all mothers when you read this and together we can help each other!

The reading at the top of the page is a prayer and the bottom an affirmation for your child to feel confident!

It's time for bed, sweet child.

You are so loved!

Let's pray, before you sleep.

You are so special to God!

4

Dear God, help me to be nice to everyone. To all my friends and family.

You are so kind!

6

Help me be a good helper
for mom and dad.

You are a hard worker!

God, be by my side, and help me
not to be scared of anything!

You are so courageous!

Thank you for our house and
all our food to eat.

You are so blessed!

Help me close my eyes
and fall asleep. Amen

Everything will be just fine!

14

Mom and dad will turn
off the lights now.

You are so brave!

If you can't sleep, please don't cry! Why not try counting instead? One…two…three…four…five… six…seven…eight…nine…ten…

You are so smart!

Night, night my sweet child!
God loves you and so do we!

You are beautiful just
the way you are!

THE END....

Printed in the United States
by Baker & Taylor Publisher Services